Aseptic Production

An introduction for life scientists

Dr CF Harrison

Harrison Scientific

Copyright 2016 Dr CF Harrison. All rights reserved. No part of this publication may be reproduced, stored in a retrieval system, or transmitted, in any form or in any means – by electronic, mechanical, photocopying, recording or otherwise – without prior written permission.

So why learn about aseptic processing?

Simple molecules are boring and out of date, cries the pharmaceutical industry, the future lies in the world of biological therapeutics – targeted antibodies, engineered proteins, DNA replacement, reprogrammed cells. Vast amounts of money are being spent on biologicals every day, and every day new jobs are posted looking for people to work in the field.

Sensitive and easy to degrade, these therapeutics are produced using aseptic processing lines – designed to keep sensitive sterile drugs away from filthy, bacteria-covered things like you, dear reader. Highly complex, heavily regulated, aseptic production lines have their own language and their own world of confusing terminology. Complex terminology that you'll have to learn, if you want to get ahead in the world of biological therapeutics – whether you're in QA, production, regulatory affairs, anything really.

Not sure why your co-workers are complaining about smoke studies? No idea what a media-fill is? Can't figure out why everyone is so stressed about problems with the batch records? Confused by all of this terminology? We've got you covered.

Whether you've just started working with biological products or are preparing for your first interview, this book will give you the foundational knowledge you need to understand the complex world of aseptic production. So read on!

Table of Contents

So why learn about aseptic processing? 2
Table of Contents 3
The Basics: What is Aseptic Production? 5
Building a wall: Isolation from the external environment 7
    Clean Zones: How clean is clean? 8
    Clean Zones: The Critical Area 9
        Clean zones within clean zones: Isolator systems 10
        Complete isolation: Blow-fill-seal Methods 11
    'Supporting' clean zones 12
    Separating clean zones: Process optimisation 13
    Separating clean zones: Air Filtration 13
    Separating clean zones: Control of air flow 15
Sterilise Everything: Controlling the sterility of the aseptic line 17
    Sterilising the production line and equipment 17
        Line sterility: Steam sterilisation 18
        Line sterility: Disinfection 19
    Sterilising drug components 19
    Sterilising containers and closures 20
        Container/closure sterility: Controlling Endotoxins 22
Characterisation and Validation: Knowing that your processes work . 24
    Media fill studies 25
        Media fill studies: How often and how much? 26
        Media fill studies: The media itself 27
        Media fill studies: Incubation and contamination 28
    Validating sterilisation processes 29

    Sterilisation validation: Equipment controls and instrument calibration 31

  Filter Validation 31

    Filter validation: Post-validation testing 33

  Hold time studies 33

Records, records, records: Continuous testing and documentation 35

  Batch Records: Recording Everything You Did 35

  Training: Are your people qualified? 36

  Environmental monitoring 38

    Environmental monitoring: Monitoring methods for monitors ... 39

    Environmental monitoring: Identifying your contaminants 40

  Post-production sterility testing 40

Appendix: Glossary of Terms 43

About the author 48

The Basics: What is Aseptic Production?

Different drugs have different requirements for sterility, an orally taken tablet has a lower requirement than an inhalable powder, for example, due to the essentially 'dirtier' nature of the stomach compared to the lungs. Some products, in particular those which are intended to be injected, need to be very sterile indeed – after all, injecting bacteria directly into your body is an excellent way to get very sick very quickly. Killing patients is a very real danger with these types of drugs, and so manufacturers and regulators spend a lot of time, money and effort on ensuring the final drug is as sterile as humanly possible.

There are two general ways to make a sterile product, known as **terminal sterilisation** and **aseptic processing**. In terminal sterilisation the **active pharmaceutical ingredient** (the drug itself) and **excipients** (everything else) are mixed and filled into containers. The container is sealed and then sterilised via heat (e.g. autoclaving) or irradiation (e.g. gamma rays). By making sterilisation the final step in the process, the effect of any stray bacteria floating through the system are minimised and the process as a whole has fairly relaxed requirements for cleanliness. For this reason terminal sterilisation is generally considered the preferred route by regulatory bodies such as the FDA, it's also significantly easier and cheaper for manufacturers.

But there are many occasions where terminal sterilisation simply doesn't work, and the most common of these occurs when you are making biological therapeutics. Biological molecules such as proteins are, obviously, not particularly effective after being autoclaved, and so alternative methods to guarantee sterility are needed. The answer to this problem is known as aseptic processing or aseptic production. Here all of the components (drug, excipient, and container) are sterilised separately, mixed, and filled into containers under conditions of absolute cleanliness. This is *much* more difficult than the terminal sterilisation approach, requiring rigorous controls and testing at every stage – and thus also costs an awful lot more.

Aseptic production relies on four basic pillars: A barrier against the outside world, a solid sterilisation approach, a whole lot of tests, and a whole lot of documentation. We'll go through all of these components in the course of this book.

So, what does this involve? There are four basic things which need to be set up for an aseptic production line to have any chance of working properly. You need a solid barrier between the clean inside and the bacteria-filled outside world. You need to sterilise everything inside that barrier. You need to run a lot of tests to make sure that everything is sterile. And you need to document everything you do. Sounds simple, right? Wrong! As with most things, the details are complicated and a nightmare to grasp as a new employee. This book will be your introduction to the specialised world of aseptic production, particularly for those who are entering the quality or regulatory fields and finding themselves overwhelmed with jargon.

Building a wall: Isolation from the environment

A sterile line needs to be sterile, which means it needs to be carefully separated from the bacteria-filled outside world (including the bacteria-covered people who will be working on it). This is a multi-layered approach, where there will be several zones of steadily increasing cleanliness as you get closer to the production line. Outer zones may simply require clean shoes and a lab-coat, inner zones start to require hair nets and eventually full body coverings.

Clean room zones are designed to be as easy to clean and sterilise as possible – so smooth surfaces which are easy to wipe, minimal horizontal ledges which can gather dust, no unnecessary equipment, etc. This is the theoretical goal, at least, in actuality the room often ends up with random paperwork and equipment scattered around – though these are at least kept to a minimum. Potential contamination sources such as drains are also problematic and so you will rarely see a drain with a direct connection to the sewage system in a clean room.

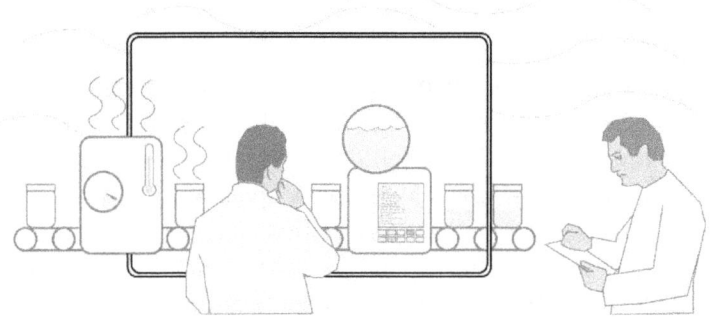

The first step in keeping your sterile product sterile is to make a barrier between it and the outside world.

Clean Zones: How clean is clean?

All of the complex interlocking filters, airflow systems, and other components of an aseptic processing line are essentially there to provide a clean zone for the filling and sealing of the sterile product. The main challenge lies in keeping the air within the clean zone free of any floating particles which could drift across and contaminate your product. But how clean is clean enough?

The American FDA and European EMA have slightly differing definitions of what is considered 'clean enough' (which are detailed in the following paragraph), but the general requirement is that each cubic metre of air in the critical zone should have less than 3520 particles greater than 0.5µm and less than one bacterium per cubic metre.

FDA recommended Action Levels for clean zones

Clean Area Classification (particles (≥0.5µm) per cubic foot)	ISO Designation (ISO14644-1)	Equivalent particles (≥0.5µm) per m³	Microbes (in CFU) per m³ via active measuring	Microbes (in CFU) per 90mm plate via settling measurement
100	5	3250	1	1
1000	6	35200	7	3
10000	7	352000	10	5
100000	8	3520000	100	50

Ok, so what does this table mean? The US system uses a Clean Area Classification system based on the number of particles allowed per cubic foot – specifically particles which are greater than 0.5µm in size. As in almost every sphere of life, there is an ISO (International Standards Association) standard which applies here, and in this case the ISO designations exactly correspond to the US system. However as most countries outside the US use metric measurements, the equivalent particle count per cubic metre is also provided.

Building a wall: Isolation from the environment

The FDA also provides recommended **action levels** for microbial numbers, this can be thought of as the number of microbes which can be detected before some sort of corrective action should be taken. These are measured in **colony forming units** (CFU), basically counting how many bacterial colonies form on a plate, and are provided for both active measurement methods (sucking air into a machine and blowing it over an agar plate) and settling methods (leaving an agar plate open on the shelf for 4 hours and seeing what grows).

EMA recommended limits for microbial contamination

Grade	Air sample (CFU/m³)	Settle plates (90mm plate) CFU/4h settling	Contact plates (55mm) CFU/plate	Particles (0.5μm) per m³	Particle (5μm) per m³
A	<1	<1	<1	3520	20
B	10	5	5	3520	29
C	100	50	25	352000	2900
D	200	100	50	3520000	29000

The European health authority, EMA, uses a slightly different set of rules which cover both particle levels and microbial levels in various locations. However the Grade A designation of the clean room is effectively identical to the FDA ISO 5 with respect to particle numbers and microbial limits. The majority of pharmaceutical manufacturers will attempt to cover both of these classification systems so as to easily export to both major markets.

Clean Zones: The Critical Area

The most important of the clean zones is known as the **critical area**, it's the part of the line where the sterile drug product is filled into containers and sealed. Why critical? Because the containers are usually open to the atmosphere here, so any problems in this zone will lead to contamination of the final product. This would be Very Bad, and so there are stringent design requirements and monitoring systems set up to ensure that the critical area is as sterile as possible.

The first step in ensuring sterility involves reducing the amount of microscopic particles (and their associated bacteria). The FDA has a basic requirement that critical areas match what is known as Class 100 (ISO 5) cleanliness levels – this means that there must be less than 100 particles larger than $0.5\mu m$ in size in every cubic foot of air.

How is this actually achieved? Through a combination of very good air filtration and really strenuous control of the cleanliness and quality of the entire zone. However the older approach of setting aside an entire room as a critical area has problems, workers still have to enter and exit (bringing bacteria along) and the room itself can be difficult to keep as clean as necessary. To avoid these problems, many companies are moving towards protecting the entire line with a covering known as a *barrier isolator*.

Clean zones within clean zones: Isolator systems

An **isolator** or isolation system takes yet another step towards total sterility for the critical area. What is it? A barrier isolator is essentially a big shell which covers the entire production line and prevents any external bacteria or particles from reaching the open containers. The shell itself is usually made of glass and stainless steel, both of which are tough and easy to clean, though other materials such as tough plastic are sometimes used. Isolators are both more secure and easier to keep sterile than the 'critical zone/room' approach, and so is commonly found in most modern pharmaceutical production lines

Isolators can be completely closed, in which case all materials are loaded in via airlock or prior to production. Alternatively, and more commonly, they can have small entry/exit gaps known as *mouse-holes* for materials and filled containers to pass through. Closed isolators tend to be more tolerant of turbulent and chaotic airflow – everything is sealed and so particle movement is less of

Building a wall: Isolation from the environment

a problem. By contrast open isolators are always bringing new material in and thus need to ensure that the airflow follows a single path with minimal turbulence or dead zones.

In either case the isolator will protect the entire line from contamination via positive pressure (where the internal pressure is higher than the external pressure) so that any cracks/gaps which are present lead to outwards leaks, i.e. no particles will enter the sterile zone. This overpressure normally has to be between 20-50 Pascals, which provides a gentle airflow rather than a roaring wind (for reference, the 'standard' pressure at sea level is about 100 kilopascal, so it's not a *large* pressure difference). This is helped by clever design of the entry/exit ports to prevent turbulence which could eddy particles back into the sterile region. As with the critical zone described previously, the inside of an isolator needs to be kept at Class 100/ISO 5, though the surrounding zone can go all the way down to Class 100,000/ISO 8 if well designed.

Even though an isolator shell is present, the production line will still have mechanical difficulties, jams, etc. To let workers fix any stoppages and perform interventions, the isolator will have rubber/plastic gloves hanging inside the shell – people can then simply reach into them to work in the sterile zone. As the gloves are less durable than the plastic barrier, they are a potential source of contamination and thus are regularly tested for integrity and sterility. Beyond this isolators need to be decontaminated and sterilised using the same processes as would be used for a 'normal' critical zone and processing line.

Complete isolation: Blow-fill-seal Methods

Blow-fill-seal (BFS) is a fairly clever manufacturing process which lets you make, fill, and then close a container without it ever coming in contact with the outside environment. Because of this, BFS methods are considered to be very useful in the pharmaceutical world and are often used for aseptic products such as eye-drops. The technique is, however, less common for injectable biologics due to worries about compounds leaching from the plastic and affecting protein stability.

How does it work? First a plastic resin such as polyethylene/polypropylene is heated and extruded (pushed through) a small hole, making a long, hanging tube known as a parison. The parison is placed within a mould and cut away from the main machine, then transferred to another part where a filling needle (or mandrel) is inserted into the tube. By pumping air in, the still-warm plastic will form the shape provided by the mould (i.e. a bottle or container), and the same needles will then fill the container with the drug/excipient solution. The top of the container can then be sealed through more heat and the final sterile, sealed container is ready for packaging. An excellent example of a BFS-product is the single-use saline solution which is often used for cleaning out eyes or wounds – opened by ripping the plastic apart but sterile until that point.

As with isolators and critical zones, BFS machines needs to be regularly tested and validated to ensure that they are working correctly and reach the correct sterility/particle level (once again, Class 100/ISO 5 is a minimum requirement). Beyond that they have their own specialised problems: the machine needs to avoid creating too many plastic particles during the cutting and filling steps; the heat involved in sealing can lead to drug degradation; catching containers with minor leaks can be very difficult; etc. etc. Nonetheless, BFS systems are rapidly gaining market share in the US and European pharmaceutical manufacturing facilities, so it is likely you will run into one at some stage in your career.

'Supporting' clean zones

Supporting zones are those found around the critical zone, and are usually where all of the unsterilized containers and not-yet-filtered components are stored before being sterilised and moved into the critical zone. A hopper full of glass cartridges which feeds into the irradiator would be a supporting clean zone, for example, as would the space for workers to move around the isolated filling line. This region has to be set up to minimise the potential for contaminants to enter the critical zone, thus it usually must be kept at Class 1000 (ISO 6) or Class 10,000 (ISO 7) cleanliness levels. In practice this involves many of the same approaches as used in the critical zone, albeit at a lower level.

Separating clean zones: Process optimisation

An important part of maintaining sterility involves manufacturing process optimisation. In every production zone, you will have materials and people moving around, going from one section to another, entering, exiting. It's important that the 'flow' of these is designed in a way that is efficient – e.g. you need to avoid unnecessary movement or passing of objects from one side of the zone to the other, this leads to more activity and thus higher contamination risks. As a part of this, aseptic zones try to minimise the number of people present, usually via heavy use of automation. Automation is used in the sense of having a single continuous line which takes the materials in at the start and then delivers the finished, sealed product at the end – all measurements and checks are done by the line itself without needing manual checks. Naturally this isn't perfect, something always goes wrong, and when this happens the line will be stopped while someone uses the built-in gloves to clear the jam without interrupting the sterility of the critical zone.

The other way to minimise activity and potential contamination involves controlling the number of transfers in/out of the zone. For people, that means that most of the workers will enter at the start of the shift, usually through a double-door or airlock, completely gowned, masked, and with hairnets (also beard-nets, you'll sometimes see men needing several if the beard is impressive enough). There is always a set process on how to enter the clean zone – so gloves here, hairnet there, now step over here, etc., and this will be written down in case the FDA asks to see it. Materials (the drug, the containers, etc.) will also be brought in as large batches to prevent too many entry/exit cycles.

Separating clean zones: Air Filtration

The best-sealed isolator in the world is utterly useless if you are filling it with microbe-laden air, and this is where filtration comes in. There are two major types of filter, membrane filters and HEPA filters, both of which have different jobs.

Membrane filters are made of polymer layers with many pores (each of a defined size) which act to filter out any particles which are larger than the pore size. The rate at which they work is usually too low to make them worthwhile as a general air filtration system, and so they are usually used to filter compressed gas (air, nitrogen, carbon dioxide, etc.) for use in cleaning lines, adding airflow or gas overlays to certain sections, etc. Membrane filters can occasionally have condensation forming as moisture in the gas being filtered precipitates onto the filter – most production lines will thus try to heat the filter to prevent this condensation from occurring.

HEPA filters (high-efficiency particulate arresting) are essentially a chaotic mat of fibreglass fibres which blocks particles flowing through the filter – the general requirement is that they stop over 99.97% of all the particles present at the inlet. People coming from a life science background will probably have worked with HEPA filters before, as they form an essential part of the clean/sterile bench for lab work.

HEPA filters supply the majority of the clean air which is used in the clean zone, and thus have regular testing to verify that they are working as they should. There are two types of test which are performed, **leak testing** and **efficiency testing**. Efficiency testing is a general check for the rating of the filter, is it capable of stopping the required 99.97% of >0.3µm particles? How much better than that basic requirement is it? Leak testing, by contrast, is a regular check of the *filter and housing* to make sure it is up to scratch and makes a tight seal. This is done by spraying an aerosol such as dioctylphthalate (water is never used as it may encourage microbial growth – which would be bad) into one side of the filter. The spraying method used is carefully controlled to make sure that there are many 0.3µm particles, with a wide coverage of the entire inlet. A photometer or equivalent probe is then (figuratively) waved over the filter to see how much of that initial spray passed through the filter, anything more than 0.01% getting through is considered a 'leak' and thus calls for replacement of the filter. Leak testing is usually done at least twice a year in the aseptic production rooms, though can be more often if the line is having problems.

Beyond leak testing, HEPA filters are also checked for the velocity of air which passes through them – the general idea here is that a filter with variations in airflow will lead to turbulence down the line, and this in turn can lead to contamination. All of these tests are usually done by a contract company (smoke testing in particular requires extremely specialised equipment), but the responsibility to do everything correctly *always* remains with the manufacturer.

Separating clean zones: Control of air flow

So how exactly do you keep your critical area separate from your clean zone and your clean zone from your surrounding area? The majority of the system is sealed, but there are gaps in the airtight system – if nothing else you need inlets for the drug, excipients, and containers, and an outlet where the filled and sealed containers can exit. A major component of a clean zone is the steady airflow which flows from the critical zone outwards to the less clean zones. This is achieved by pumping filtered air into the critical zone to cause a higher pressure region, which then forces the air out through the inlet/outlet gaps, taking any microscopic particles and associated bacteria with it. This same approach applies to the doors which let workers into the supporting zones, the clean zone has a higher pressure than the external area and so helps to blow dust out when the doors are opened.

To make sure that a sufficient 'breeze' is set up at these gaps, the zone also needs to have a lot of air coming in – the rule of thumb is that the lowest clean zone (ISO 8) should have enough airflow that all of the air in the zone is changed over 20 times per hour – more critical zones need even more. The airflow is also designed to blow in a set direction, usually with the aim of moving any possible particles away from the filling area. Generally a critical area will avoid eddies of air or 'stagnant' zones where there is no flow, as these can lead to particles or microbes building up to unwanted concentrations.

Verifying all of these air flow requirements leads to one of the most boring jobs you can have in aseptic production quality assurance – smoke studies. Picture a number of people standing in the aseptic production room, standing very, very still, while a machine makes a thin, fragile stream of smoke. Video cameras watch this stream of smoke as it wends its way through the system, tracing out the airflow. Sounds kind of interesting, and it is, the first time. Then the smoke machine is moved slightly, and they do it again. And again. Smoke studies are a vital part of validating the efficiency of your air-flow control, but they are certainly not, well… exciting.

Sterilise Everything: Aseptic line sterility

Filters, isolators, controlled airflow. All of these allow you to isolate the critical zone from the external environment and its associated microbes. But isolation is not enough, the line needs to be completely free of any microbes which could be present in the equipment, the containers, even the drug itself. This is guaranteed by **sterilisation**, the process of killing all microbes present, and different techniques are used for the equipment, the containers, and the drug components.

Sterile environments require sterilisation – what a surprise!

Sterilising the production line and equipment

It's a sterile production line, and so it needs to be sterile. Fair enough, but high quality filters and air control aren't enough to keep the critical zone microbe-free – it needs to be regularly sterilised to kill anything which may be growing. The same applies to equipment, containers, and closures. Generally an aseptic line will do a thorough sterilisation between each batch (usually just before production starts) and the line will be kept sealed and microbe-free until production begins.

The basic requirement for sterilisation processes is that they provide a **sterilisation assurance level** of 10^{-6}. What does this mean? We can never state with complete certainty that the process has worked perfectly, so this number this is the probability that any given 'sterilised' object will, in fact, not be sterile. Thus a sterilisation assurance level of 10^{-6} can be read as saying that one out of every million runs will fail. If we assume one sterilisation run per day, this would be a single failure in every ~2700 years, which is usually considered a negligible level of risk.

Line sterility: Steam sterilisation

Steam sterilisation is one of the most commonly used methods in the medical and biotech fields, you've undoubtedly had experience with it in the form of a laboratory-scale autoclave. Steam can be used as a method for sterilising equipment which is separate from the production line (by placing the equipment into a contained autoclave) or to clean the entire line at once (which is known as Sterilisation-in-Place, or SIP).

The major advantage of steam-based systems is that they can reach and sterilise all exposed surfaces, making it particularly useful for sterilisation-in-place processes. However, this means that sections which are somehow cut off from the steam supply may not be properly sterilised – for example filters installed in piping will cause very significant drops in pressure and temperature on the down-stream side, which leads to reduced effectiveness. Similarly, autoclaves need to be able to remove the existing air from the chamber prior to adding sterilising steam, lest the majority of the heat energy be passed on to the air, not the equipment to be sterilised.

Different microbes have different levels of resistance to sterilisation, and so the autoclave cycle needs to be able to kill all of these – normally this involves a cycle of 134°C for 3-5 minutes or the lower 121°C for 15 minutes (highly resistant thermophilic archaea can survive these temperatures, but are a fairly rare sight outside of thermal springs).

Line sterility: Disinfection
Usually used as a secondary technique alongside steam sterilisation, disinfection is the process of using chemical treatment to kill any microbes which are present. Disinfectants target surface-borne microbes and vary widely in their effectiveness and costs – some can kill basically everything, some are less effective against bacterial spores, some are incredibly toxic and need careful checks to make sure nothing slips through into the drug being produced. Bacterial spores are particularly challenging as they are resistant to many widely used disinfectants, to avoid this most disinfection programs use a combination of chemicals to ensure sterility.

All disinfectants being used in the aseptic processing line need to be checked for efficacy before use, a process which often falls under the remit of QC and laboratory controls. Generally this involves testing that the disinfectant can kill all of the microbes which are regularly found in the facility – there is usually no point in ensuring that you can kill rare pathogens from the highlands of Papua New Guinea if you are extremely unlikely to have these bacteria in the facility. The effectiveness of the general disinfection process is then followed through standard environmental monitoring programs.

Sterilising drug components
A **drug component** is the term usually used to refer to the ingredients used to manufacture the final drug product – this can refer to the active pharmaceutical ingredient (API), the excipients (non-active parts of the final drug), even the water used to solubilise everything (this is commonly known as 'Water for Injection', or WFI).

The actual sterilisation process used varies from component to component – stable components such as chemical powders are often sterilised via dry heat or irradiation. Biological molecules such as proteins, however, will fall apart rapidly when heated and so need to be sterilised by gentler methods. A very common technique is to take the drug and excipient components, dissolve them in sterile water, and then filter the entire mix. Known as filter sterilisation, this usually involves passing the mix through a pre-filter (which pulls out the larger junk in the solution) followed by several filters with pore sizes <0.2μm (to remove as many microbes as possible). The solution after these filter steps is considered 'sterile' and ready to be filled into containers.

Filter sterilisation is one of the most important parts of the production process, and so is usually considered a 'critical' parameter – one where problems can have major effects on the final product. Samples will usually be taken from the post-filtration solution to check for **bioburden**, the amount of microbes present in the solution (there should be none, as you'd hope). The filter is also tested after use for integrity (i.e. no holes or tears), this is usually done by **bubble point** testing which measures the pressure at which bubbles pass through the filter, directly related to the pore size. Problems with either of these tests will lead to major investigations and often to the dumping of the entire batch.

Sterilising containers and closures

It's all very well have a clean zone with exceptional sterility, but if the drug is in a filthy container then it's all just wasted effort. Thus any aseptic production line has to ensure that the containers and closures are sterilised before entering the critical zone and then are kept sterile until sealed.

Often described together, there is nonetheless a difference between **containers** (such as a glass jar) and **closures** (such as the jar lid). Containers and closures perform the same function for pharmaceuticals as for marmalade, as long as they remain unopened the contents should be as sterile as when it was manufactured. Much like marmalade, many sterile pharmaceuticals are filled into glass cartridges or vials – glass is relatively easy to clean and sterilise and has far less leaching of compounds into the liquid it holds compared to, say, plastic. Unlike marmalade jars, pharmaceutical-quality glass has very extensive quality controls and a correspondingly impressive price tag.

Sterilising containers/closures occurs in multiple steps, and begins with the pre-sterilisation wash/rinse cycles using high-quality water – this is intended to wash away the majority of contaminants which may still be present. Glass containers are then usually sterilised via 'dry heat', this method is different to the autoclaving which most life scientists are familiar with as it uses very hot, almost moisture-free air instead of steam. Dry heat is preferred for several reasons, it does not require post-sterilisation drying time (which makes it faster), and the treatment also serves to break down any bacterial endotoxins which may be on the containers (which means that no second step is required).

If the container is made of another material, such as plastic, then sterilisation becomes slightly more difficult. Gamma irradiation is one option, but treatment with toxic gases (such as ethylene oxide) is more common thanks to the ease of treating all exposed surfaces of the container. It does have the disadvantage of leaving behind residues (both ethylene oxide and its assorted by-products), the levels of these are tested as part of the standard monitoring process.

Closures are very often made of rubber, as it is relatively cheap and provides an excellent seal. As they are poor conductors of heat, rubber stoppers don't sterilise properly under dry heat, (they also melt occasionally, which can be embarrassing). Because of this rubber closures are usually washed multiple times, then sterilised with steam (i.e. autoclaving) or irradiation. The washing process will also help to break down endotoxins, provided the water is hot enough, though this needs to be verified by constant testing.

Containers and closures are often 'siliconised', coated with a thin layer of silicone to provide a further barrier between the drug and the container or closure. Silicone tends to break down around

350°C and so adds an upper limit to the amount of heat which can be used in sterilising these treated materials.

Container/closure sterility: Controlling Endotoxins

Microbes are, well, microbes, but what are **endotoxins**? These are large fat/polysaccharide containing molecules which make up the outer membrane of many bacteria. They cause a very strong immune response in animals, sometimes strong enough to lead to septic shock, organ failure, and death. Endotoxins are a particular problem for biological drugs, the majority are both made from bacterial sources and intended to be injected (which can lead to very rapid septic shock). Because of this, endotoxin controls and specifications are a major focus for biological manufacturers, covering both the final product and the raw materials which are used to create it.

Excessive endotoxin levels in injectable drugs can lead to the patient undergoing septic shock, an overpowered immune response which can cause organ shutdown and death. The 'acceptable' level for endotoxins in any one injection is also quite variable, what may cause a minor swelling in an adult can seriously harm a child or someone receiving multiple injections. Because of this, the prevention and destruction of endotoxins is a major focus for injectable pharmaceuticals manufacturers and is considered a basic part of Good Manufacturing Practice.

As mentioned in the container/closure system, the most effective method for destroying endotoxin contaminants is via high-temperature dry heat sterilisation, although high-temperature water washes are also an acceptable method. 'Moist heat' sterilisation (i.e. autoclaving) is not effective enough to rely on, similarly endotoxin molecules will pass directly through a standard sterile filtration setup.

Because of these factors, dry heat is the most commonly used sterilisation/depyrogenisation combination method, allowing for faster processes and thus speedier production. The process of breaking down endotoxins, known as depyrogenisation, is a requirement for all injectable products and is strongly recommended for most others. It's tested by 'painting' test containers with endotoxin solutions and then seeing how much is left after treatment – the FDA usually requires at least a 99.9% reduction.

Characterising and Validating Processes

Producing even a single vial of sterile biological requires the combination of many different processes, all of which need to work together flawlessly. Before any production starts these processes need to be trialled and tested, to make sure that they work consistently and well.

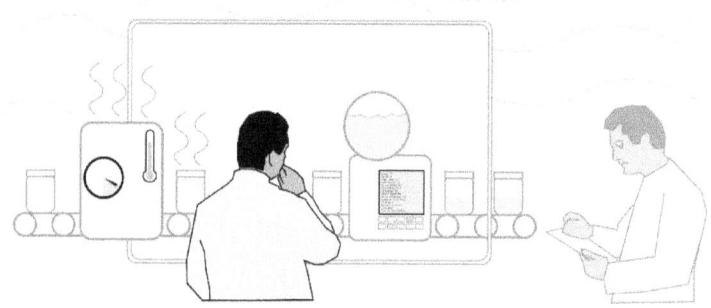

How can you be certain that your processes are reliable and accurate? Test, test, and test some more.

The formal term for this is **process validation,** the act of gathering a lot of data from many different points of your process to show that, despite variation in your starting materials, the final product is of a reproducibly high quality. It's a very complicated topic, especially when it involves validating changes being made to an FDA/EMA-approved process, and so this book will concentrate on the validation of an aseptic production line. For more details on the complex world of change control and process characterisation/validation, please see the other books in this series.

Characterising and Validating Processes

There are many types of studies which need to be performed. Some of the most important study types are listed here

Type of Study	Investigates…
Media Fill	Does the filling process and associated sterilisation let any microbes get through to contaminate the drug product?
Sterilisation validation	Does the method used to sterilise the line or equipment consistently kill all microbes which are present?
Filter validation	Does the sterile filter actually screen out all microbes which may be present?
Hold time studies	Where can we pause the process without having problems, and if so, for how long?

There is a difference between qualification and validation. **Qualification** is the process of ensuring that the equipment you are using is *capable* of working to the quality level which is required (this is sometimes also known as *verification*). **Validation** is the process of *documenting* that your processes provide required level of quality.

In other words – *things are qualified, processes are validated*. The first step is to qualify your sterilisation equipment to ensure that it is capable of sterilising the equipment, zone, containers, etc. These tests are repeated on a period basis, known as requalification, to make sure the equipment remains in acceptable shape. Once initial qualification is done, the processes which use this equipment are validated, documenting that the sterilisation methods work.

Media fill studies

Sometimes called 'process simulation' but more often referred to as a **media fill study**, this is a full scale trial run of the production process which uses growth media instead of drug/excipient. Once sealed, the containers are then incubated to see if any microbial growth occurs – if yes, then there is a good chance that contamination could occur during normal production runs, obviously a bad thing. A media fill study is an extensive undertaking, it needs to match reality as closely as possible while still covering all the myriad potential failures which could occur.

Every media fill you will be involved in will begin with the design document or protocol, which will go over what is being examined and how it will be examined. The overall intention is to simulate an actual production run as closely as possible, right down to how people react when something goes wrong. From a reality point of view, each study needs to use the actual containers that would normally be filled, the line must run at its normal speed and with the normal settings, any shift changes which would normally occur also need to happen during the media fill – the study even needs to somehow simulate factors such as operator tiredness at the end of a shift and the various interventions which occur when workers need to stop and fix a problem.

All of this needs to be documented in a study-specific batch record as well as in the final study report, which will be signed by representatives from several departments. If there were any problems, (such as contamination or unreliable results), then quality assurance will need to perform an investigation to find out what the underlying cause of the problem was. Depending on the cause of the problem, your line may need to repeat the media fill several times. Even if there are no problems, a successful media fill is not a direct tick of approval for a process – authorities will not accept a media fill study as proof that a slightly dodgy practice is acceptable, the requirement to avoid contamination risks where possible remains regardless.

Media fill studies: How often and how much?
How often do you need to perform a media fill study? As with most things, the answer is 'it depends'. When the line has just been installed, several media fills will be performed as part of the initial qualification – this helps to show that the overall process is reproducible. Once qualified and running, media fills are performed several times a year, with anyone who is part of the

Characterising and Validating Processes   27

critical/clean zone having to participate in at least one media fill per year.

Media fill studies will simulate the 'typical' interventions which may occur – stopping the line, fixing jams, waiting a while as the power is fixed, etc. These will usually involve throwing several half-filled cartridges away, and you'll need to document how many were discarded as well (auditors tend to get suspicious when 100 vials suddenly disappear in the middle of a study). There is no requirement to do these interventions each time the media fill study is performed, instead most studies will change the occurrence base on rarity – a common intervention will be simulated every time, something uncommon may only be simulated once per year.

As well as aiming to simulate the possible interventions which may come up, media fill studies are intended to match how long an actual production run will take. This means that if your normal process takes several shifts to get everything bottled up, then the media fill should also take several shifts, and should include all of the chaos that occurs when people enter and exit the clean zones.

The *size* of the media fill batch doesn't need to be the same as the standard batches, but should be enough to 'accurately simulate' the standard size. In practice, this means that 5000-10000 units (vials, cartridges) is a good minimum starting point, processes with a low level of automation will need to have more units to be persuasive – often up to the normal batch size.

Media fill studies: The media itself

It's a media fill study so you need to fill things with media, but which media? Most studies will use soybean casein digest media, a generalist media which lets pretty much all contaminants grow quite happily. Other growth media are possible, such as those designed for anaerobic microbes or specific contaminants, but these are usually done as an additional test on top of the standard media fill. Regardless of what is chosen, there need to be positive and negative controls – positives are cartridges inoculated with a very low number of bacteria to prove that the media chosen actually supports microbial growth. The idea of deliberately adding bacteria to aseptic lines tends to horrify most drug manufacturers, though the general attitude of the FDA can be summarised as "a) it's a requirement and b) your cleaning procedures should be killing everything afterwards anyway".

Media fill studies: Incubation and contamination

Once all of the cartridges, vials, etc. have been filled and sealed, they are packed away in and incubated for at least two weeks to see if anything grows. The incubation temperature has to be between 20-35°C to allow the growth of as many different species as possible (this tends to catch many life scientists out – we're no longer just growing *E. coli*!).

Once the two weeks (or longer) is up, every single cartridge is checked for contamination by either a member of the quality control (QC) group or a worker with QC oversight. This is about as boring as you can imagine, but it has to be done. Any cartridge with a hint of growth is immediately passed off to the resident QC microbiologist who will then set about identifying the contaminant (down to the species level) and determining where it came from. The general assumption of health authorities is that a properly set-up aseptic manufacturing line will have essentially zero contamination events. If a single 'sterile' cartridge with microbial growth is observed, then this will need to be the subject of a thorough investigation (and possibly even require a repeat of the whole process, see the table below). This also applies across multiple media fill studies – if you observe an intermittent problem with contamination, then there is likely an underlying problem which needs to be investigated. Given that contamination results usually come several weeks after a media fill, the production line has likely seen several other manufacturing campaigns – QC will also need to determine if there is a risk to these other products as well.

Required actions following microbial growth during a media fill study

Number of units being filled	Contaminated units found	Required actions
< 5000	One	Investigation of the cause, then revalidation of the line
5000 to 10000	One	Investigation of the cause, and potentially a repeat of the media fill study
	Two	Investigation of the cause, then revalidation of the line
> 10000	One	Investigation of the cause
	Two	Investigation, then revalidation of the line

As you can see, there are very strict limits on how many contaminants can be observed before the entire run needs to be repeated or the line needs to be revalidated. This is entirely in keeping with the requirements for the final drug product – if a drug is labelled as sterile but contains a non-sterile unit, the manufacturer is liable for some very hefty punishment.

Validating sterilisation processes

It's not enough to think that your sterilisation process works, you have to know it. Sterilisation validation tests are regularly performed to ensure that the techniques being used are, in fact, up to the job. As previously mentioned, the process should provide a sterilisation assurance level of 10^{-6} – on average one out of every million runs will fail.

The first step is to *qualify* your sterilisation equipment to ensure that it is capable of sterilising the equipment, zone, containers, etc. These tests are repeated on a period basis, known as requalification, to make sure the equipment remains in acceptable shape. First comes **mapping studies**, where temperature or pressure sensors are scattered throughout the equipment (autoclaves, pipes, etc.) to check whether the conditions are the same throughout. An example of this would be scattering temperature sensors throughout an empty filling line, then running a full sterilisation-in-place cycle. Was the required temperature reached everywhere, even in hard-to-reach pipes? Mapping studies need to show that the conditions are uniform in every part being treated.

Next comes **heat penetration studies**, which look at the efficacy of the sterilisation when the equipment is loaded (e.g. a filled autoclave, for example). A filled system has more mass which needs to be heated, as well as more potential 'dead zones' which may be cut off from the sterilisation, thus penetration studies will be needed to show that the system works under real-life conditions. These studies usually use temperature sensors paired with biological indicators (basically a container or strip of microbes which will grow if the process fails). As with the mapping studies, these are scattered throughout the system, but examine both the sterilising equipment *and* the materials being sterilised. They tend to focus on parts with a higher risk of problems – filters, pumps, tightly-wrapped or sealed objects, long tubes or pipes, etc.

Once initial qualification is done, the processes which use this equipment are validated, documenting that the sterilisation methods work. This involves repeating a standard sterilisation program on at least three separate occasions, checking that no living microbes are detected after the run. Normally several different loads will be checked, including the **empty load** (where the system is, well, empty) and the **worst-case load** (where the system has the maximum number of difficult-to-sterilise objects present). If your program passes the validation runs, then it is considered safe to use for routine production.

Validation studies are repeated periodically, usually every year at least. They are also redone when there are major changes in the method or settings used – for example, switching from a 15 minute autoclave sterilisation cycle to a 10 minute one will require a revalidation of the entire process. This is a major undertaking (and one with heavy regulatory requirements) so changes to sterilisation are not performed lightly.

Sterilisation validation: Equipment controls and instrument calibration

All of the complex and expensive studies described in the previous section are completely useless if the sensors being used aren't working properly – this applies in both validation and in general use. To avoid this kind of thing, instruments need to be regularly tested and calibrated according to written procedures.

What sort of testing? Depends on the instrument. Temperature sensors are calibrated using environments with known temperatures at regular intervals, more often when performing validation studies. Biological indicators such as spore strips are regularly checked to make sure the microbes are actually alive before they are sterilised. Manufacturers will also often determine the **D-value** of the spore strip when a new batch arrives. The D-value or 'decimal reduction time', is time or dosage of treatment required to kill 90% of the microorganisms present, these values are always provided by spore strip/biological indicator manufacturers but will usually be double-checked before they are used.

Filter Validation

The majority of aseptic processes use filtration to remove any microbial contaminants from the liquid drug solution, usually with several filters in a row to ensure complete sterility at the end of the process step. Thus (as you would guess) the efficacy of the filter also needs to be validated, in a process which is *separate* to the media fill study discussed in the previous section.

Filter validation studies consist of 'microbial challenges', essentially putting a lot of bacteria on one side of the filter system and seeing if any make it through. The most common species used is *Brevundimonas diminuta*, a Gram-negative proteobacteria which has a diameter of about 0.3μm – the small size makes it a good challenge to 0.2μm sterile filters and will easily fit through any oversized pores in the filter membrane. Validation studies can use other microbes (e.g. environmental isolates) but will have to justify why this choice is 'as good or better' than *B. diminuta*.

The size of the filter will determine how many microbes are added to one side, with 10^7 microbes per square centimetre being the 'standard' amount. This is ridiculously high compared to any realistic contamination in normal production, but filter validation is generally intended to use the worst-case options. As with media fill studies, a 'sterile' filtrate should be perfectly sterile – no bacteria should be detected after the sterile filtration step.

There are a lot of different factors which need to be considered when putting together a filter validation test, not just the type and amount of bacteria being added to one side of the system. For example, is your drug product solution actually bactericidal, or contain some toxic components which would kill the bacteria before they pass through the membrane? You may need to use a substitute solution to do the testing. Is the solution highly viscous? How high is the pressure and flow rate which you are using? What temperature will everything run at? All of these and more need to be simulated or explained in order to state that the filter will work as intended during manufacturing.

As previously mentioned, this is not a media fill study, it examines the filter only rather than the entire process. Because of this, the filter validation experiments are usually performed in a separate development lab area, not in the production area itself (even ignoring the disruption it would cause, this would be a terrible contamination risk to the line). The laboratory (or outsourced contract research group) will use the same filter and the same conditions as the actual production line, results from here are then extrapolated to show that the filter is 'validated' – it will provide a sterile solution when used in the production process.

Filter validation: Post-validation testing

Testing doesn't stop with the initial filter validation! The filter will be regularly checked for integrity (i.e. no holes or tears) after use; this integrity testing is usually done via the **bubble point** method, which measures the pressure needed to force bubbles out of a wet filter, this pressure is directly related to the pore size. A second common method of is known as forward flow or gas diffusion, in this case pressure allows a gas to diffuse, not bubble, through a membrane; rips in the membrane will lead to much faster gas diffusion rates. If filter damage is discovered after the filtration process then the solution will need to be refiltered (if allowed by the QA and regulatory departments) or possibly discarded entirely (with the corresponding loss of large amounts of money).

Hold time studies

As you would expect, leaving a half-made drug sitting around for a long period of time is bad for its final level of quality. To prevent this kind of thing from happening, the process will contain time limits both for general production and for **hold times**, pauses in the process. As a general example, the process (as listed in the corresponding master batch record) would show that there should be a maximum of, say, 8 hours between compounding (mixing the drug and excipients together) and filling the mix into containers. Thus would be further subdivided, saying that filling can only take one hour in total, or that filtration can take two hours. Filtration in particular requires a defined limit as microbes can, given enough time, work their way through the filter to enter the 'sterile' solution. All of these times will have to be verified with data showing that a process which takes the maximum allowed time still has acceptable products at the end.

Hold times are the amount of time which a process can be paused for, either because of problems on the line or to help align manufacturing steps. A basic example would be the post-thawing hold time – once your active antibody is thawed and ready to be mixed with the excipients, how long can you leave it in the original container before it must be added to the mixing vessel?

Hold times need to be justified from a chemical point of view (e.g. protein degradation doesn't occur) as well as a microbial point of view (e.g. growth of bacteria within the hold time remains within acceptable limits). Hold times need to be determined both at an individual level and for cumulative hold – is my protein still ok if it is held at each of these points for the maximum time allowable? As with general time limits, these numbers need to be backed up by data – in practice this involves running many different runs with longer or shorter pauses and seeing where a hold could be justified.

Records: Testing and Documenting

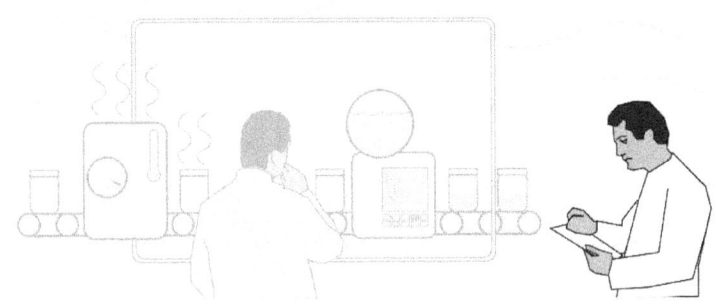

Your process needs to be continually tested and continually documented. It doesn't matter if you've done everything correctly – what isn't written down *and signed* never happened

Batch Records: Recording Everything You Did

There's a common saying which states "if it wasn't written down, it never happened." This is even more important for pharmaceuticals, where things which weren't written down *and signed correctly* are considered to never have occurred. Any production process is highly complex and has multiple things which could go wrong at any point, so keeping reliable records of everything which happened is extremely important. This is done using **batch records**.

There are two types of batch records which you will come across in your job. First are the **master batch records** (usually called MBRs), these are the instructions which will be followed in order to produce the pharmaceutical. They are very detailed and list each step from initial sterilisation through to final cleaning, as well as listing the internal codes for the materials that should be used (including filters and other 'equipment'). Beside each step will be space for recording the observation made at that point, be it a pH measurement, stirring time, even a simple check for ice in the bottle.

A single copy of this master batch record is then printed out and filled in while production goes ahead – this is known as the **executed batch record**. At the end of each page (and often at each step) the executed batch record will be signed by the person responsible for the production run, this forms a permanent record of the run. Any problems which may occur (stopping the line, needing to intervene in the automated process, etc.) will also be recorded and signed at the moment they happen.

Why is this important? Batch records serve two different but very important purposes. The master batch record says in exact detail what should be done at each point in the process, so that it always occurs in the same way. The executed batch records let you look back after the drug has been produced to see if anything went wrong (something always goes wrong), how serious it was, and whether it may have affected the final product. Written records and instructions are a basic GMP requirement and are a frequent topic when FDA/EMA/health authority inspections occur.

Training: Are your people qualified?
The ideal aseptic process is one where people aren't needed at all, it simply runs smoothly without the need for human intervention. This is, well, not very realistic – despite the best plans of process engineers, people are always required to troubleshoot and fix problems, and thus everyone working on an aseptic line has to use and understand aseptic techniques.

What exactly are aseptic techniques? It's a general term used for methods which ensure that sterile parts stay sterile. For example – sterile materials should only be touched with sterile instruments, such as sterilised pincers, and not with gloves or gowns. Similarly the materials should only be touched from the side, you should avoid reaching over the container as particles can drop from your hands. Workers should move slowly and deliberately, no running back and forth in a panic which can create turbulence and ruin the controlled airflow. People should be aware of how the airflow works, and avoid standing 'upwind' of anything important.

One major factor in sterile/aseptic technique is the use of the gown, basically a shield which protects the clean zone from your filthy, microbe-laden body. The gowns are sterilised, made of material which won't shed fluff, and very often disposable. You should probably keep in mind that 'gown' is also a generic term in SOPs and regulations for many different elements on top of the gown itself – this includes things such as face masks, gloves, beard covers, etc. Getting gowned up is a multi-stage process where you will find yourself stepping over barriers, balancing on one foot to put on the clean-room shoe-covers, putting on different glove layers at different times – all in all a very complex process and one which is always documented in a standard 'entry SOP'.

The ongoing aseptic training in also involves ongoing testing, the most common of which involves people from quality assurance taking samples from your gloves and gown to see if any microbes are present. If yes, it's usually a 'deviation' with an associated investigation, more training, requalification, even being kicked out of the clean room permanently if you have enough deviations. Glove testing is often done almost daily, other monitoring samples will be taken at a lower rate which will be given in an official monitoring plan. The people doing this testing (usually from the quality assurance group) also need to demonstrate correct aseptic technique – and so you will often see QA checking current workers and each other for microbial contamination.

This sort of knowledge doesn't get handed down in school, naturally, so everyone has to be trained in the right way to do things. As well as the initial training which is needed before even entering the clean room, there will be an ongoing training program with written proof that each worker is up-to-date. Why written? Because written training records are a basic GMP requirement (and also one of those things that are very often requested during inspections, so you really don't want to screw up here).

Environmental monitoring

An aseptic production line needs to be free of microbes (duh) and this needs to be shown via testing. Generally the responsibility of QC Microbiology, environmental monitoring is about, well, monitoring the environment. More helpfully, it involves checking for the presence of microbes in the air or on surfaces in the clean zone.

Environmental monitoring begins with a detailed written plan, which clearly indicates the locations which will be tested, how often testing will happen, how the testing will be done, etc. As you would expect, areas which are most important (those where a lot of activity occurs, or where the product is exposed to the environment) are tested more often, but testing will also occur in gowning rooms, in corridors, etc. Testing for sterility in critical areas is done *after* production is finished to prevent any potential contamination occurring, but testing of less-critical areas is usually done at the same time as production to save time.

Generally the monitoring program will have set alert levels, a limit for the amount of microbial contamination which can be seen before a full inspection needs to be done. These levels vary with the location being tested, the air inside the filling station will need to be microbe-free, the gowning room is less important. Once these alert levels are broken, however, quality assurance members will become involved to perform full evaluation, including a written report, of the incident and underlying causes (if there is an underlying cause, very often no reason can be identified).

A monitoring program is not just meant to show the current level of sterility, but also how those values compare to ones in the past. This is known as **trending** or identifying trends, and it involves examining long-term results to see if one zone is getting worse over time. If a significant trend can be seen, it will normally trigger an investigation even if the individual results are still below the alert levels. Although very important, environmental monitoring isn't perfect – some low level contamination may sneak through without being detected, or only be detected once in a while (this can be particularly irritating when occasional 'false positive' results screw up the data). Because of this, the monitoring program needs to be aware of and properly evaluate these individual spikes as well as trends in results.

Environmental monitoring: Monitoring methods for monitors

So, how is environmental monitoring actually done? There are three main methods, surface, active air, and passive air monitoring. Surface testing is simply the testing of various exposed surfaces (floors, walls, equipment, operators' gloves, etc.) to see if any microbes are present. This is done using **contact plates**, an agar plate which is designed to be easily pressed against surfaces to pick up any microbial contamination. These agar plates are then incubated to see if any colonies form.

The second main method is known as **active air monitoring**. As the name suggests, it involves actively drawing air into particle counter or microbe collector. The most common form is known as an impactor, it basically sucks air in via a pump and then blows it over a solid medium such as agar. The actual engineering is more complex than this, of course, with rotating plates and different filter sizes available, even hand-held samplers which you wave around like a noisy flashlight, but the basic principle remains the same. As a known volume of air is drawn in with use, these systems can be used to quantify the microbial burden in the air – this is a major advantage over passive systems. Because of the sheer variety of air sampling devices, the particular ones used in your aseptic production zone need to be qualified and calibrated at regular intervals.

Passive air monitoring is even simpler than active, as it involves setting agar plates out on flat surfaces and then leaving them there for a few hours. Microbes in the air will then settle onto these plates and be identified after incubation. Because they are intended to be left for several hours, care needs to be taken to make sure that the plates do not dry out (a particular problem in high airflow areas), as this will prevent microbes from growing well.

Unlike active systems, passive monitoring systems only provide qualitative information (so 'what is it' rather than 'how much') and so is usually used as a cheap and simple supporting method to active systems.

Environmental monitoring: Identifying your contaminants

So your testing has found some sort of colony forming unit, but how do you know whether this is a problem or not? This is where the laboratory characterisation comes in, where they will aim to identify any microbes which pop up during monitoring – normally to at least the genus and preferably to the species level. Traditionally this was done via biochemical/phenotypic characterisation of isolated strains, but these days everyone just sends the microbe sample for genome sequencing – this is faster and often cheaper than the old-fashioned methods. Having said that, you still need the first colony of microbes, and so plates are still incubated for long periods of time (usually 7+ days at room temperature or 2-3+ days at 30°C) to see what grows.

Microbiology QC will build a database of 'common contaminants' which occur during routine testing and will use that to help identify microbes and determine their level of risk to the final product (there will *always* be some sort of microbe picked up, that's just the way of the world). This information is then used during the following investigation to decide if the contaminant a) represents a problem to the particular batch of product affected, or b) signifies possible trend or ongoing problem with sterility, which is obviously more serious.

Post-production sterility testing

All of the effort described in this book is going into creating a sterile pharmaceutical product, with emphasis on the *sterile*. As this is such a critical requirement of the product, it is naturally something that is tested very carefully indeed.

The main challenge, however, is that you can't test every single item which is produced (else there'd be nothing left to sell). Worse than that, the number of items which are taken for sterility testing is usually fairly small, which further limits the likelihood that you will spot a contamination. If you imagine a typical batch of 10,000 sterile vials, sterility testing would often cover, say, 20 of those vials. Even if one of every thousand of those vials were packed with bacteria, you would miss them entirely in about 98% of cases. This limited sensitivity means that *any* non-sterile unit is considered a serious problem (or **deviation**) and grounds for a thorough investigation.

To try and avoid some of these problems, sterility samples are taken throughout the entire manufacturing process (start, middle and end) and often alongside any processing interventions which may stop the line. The method used to spot non-sterile units also needs to be carefully refined and validated to make sure that nothing slips through (particularly important when the product itself is antimicrobial, as this can prevent contamination from appearing until later).

Once you've found a contamination (known as a 'sterility positive') then quality assurance will move in to conduct an investigation. First comes identification of the microbe itself, usually by sequencing – is it something commonly found in the testing lab, in production, on people? If it is rare in production but common in the laboratory, it may be a mistake in the testing – this means going back to retest more samples from the batch. Next comes historical trends – is there an overall increase in contaminants seen in environmental monitoring? What about current factors for that batch – are a lot of new employees working in the zone? Are there odd results in the records which may indicate a problem during production? Working in QA is very much like being a detective – they need to sift through a lot of evidence to hunt down the underlying cause for the deviation.

Once the investigation is complete, then a deviation report and associated **Corrective and Protective Actions** (CAPAs) will be written. These state what went wrong, and what will be done in future to avoid this problem. The batch which caused all this trouble will be considered non-sterile (and thus unable to be sold) until it's completely cleared by QA. This is quite uncommon for aseptic process products and a common (but expensive) approach is to dump the batch and start again.

A Glossary of Terms

Term	Meaning
Active Air Monitoring	Using what is essentially a fancy vacuum cleaner to actively pull air across an agar plate, so as to determine how many microbes are floating around in your critical zone
Airlock	Just like on a spaceship, this is a room with two doors designed to keep one side (the outside environment) separate from the other (the clean zone). There is usually a pressure-difference across the airlock to make sure microbes are blown away from the clean zone.
Alert level	The point at which your monitoring system says 'there *may* be a problem', and which leads to closer examination of the process.
Action Level	The point (higher than an alert level) at which there *is* a problem, and where you *have to* perform an investigation.
Active Pharmaceutical Ingredient (API)	The part of your final product which has an actual pharmaceutical effect
Aseptic Production	Producing your drug in an extremely sterile environment, as opposed to terminal sterilisation. This is the usual approach taken by biological drugs.
Aseptic Processing Facility	The part of the building where aseptic production is performed, separated from the outside environment by physical barriers, air filters, etc.
Bioburden	The number of microbes which are found on an item before sterilisation (or after, depending on your process)
Biological Indicator	A group of test microbes which are placed inside the equipment while testing

	the sterilisation process – if the sterilisation has worked, these microbes should also be dead.
Blow-Fill-Seal (BFS)	A manufacturing technique where plastic containers are extruded, blown into shape, filled with sterile liquids, and then sealed – all without exposure to the outside environment.
Bubble-Point Testing	Determining the presence of defects in a liquid filter by measuring the pressure needed to force bubbles through it.
Corrective and Preventative Action (CAPA)	The outcome of a deviation investigation should be a set of actions that you will take to prevent the problem happening again – CAPAs.
Clean Zone	A subset of the aseptic facility, this is a region or room which has a set cleanliness level and which has been verified as achieving that level.
Closure	Your drug is filled into a container, which is then sealed with a closure – think of lids, rubber stoppers, etc.
Colony forming unit (CFU)	After plating out a solution onto agar, a single microbe will grow into one small colony. This is a single CFU, and is usually considered to be 'one bacteria' (though it can be more in some species which 'stick' to each other)
Component	The term used to refer to the ingredients used to manufacture the final drug product – this can refer to the API, excipients, even the water for injection.
Contact Plate	Specially designed agar plates which can be directly pressed against surfaces to pick up any microbes which may be there.
Container	The sterile drug is filled into a container, such as a vial, a pre-filled syringe, etc. which is then sealed with a closure.

A Glossary of Terms

Critical Surface	Any surface which may directly contact the sterile product or container and thus one which needs to be carefully sterilised.
Critical Area / Critical Zone	The zone in which the sterile drug product and containers are exposed to the air, and thus the part with the highest requirements for cleanliness.
Deviation	Basically: When something goes wrong, requiring an investigation.
Disinfection	The process of killing everything which may be living on the surfaces of your clean room.
D-value	The time (in minutes) which a sterilisation process needs to reduce the number of microorganisms by 90% (i.e. 1-log).
Efficiency Testing (filters)	Testing a filter to see how effective it is at removing microbes.
Excipients	Everything which is present in the final drug product which is not the active pharmaceutical ingredient.
Empty Load	A sterilisation run without any contents to be sterilised, especially used for validation of the autoclave.
Endotoxin	A molecule such as lipopolysaccharides which are found in bacterial cell walls, and which lead to very dangerous immune reactions when introduced to the body.
Executed Batch Record	The 'filled in' batch record, with all of the times, measurements, observations, etc. clearly recorded and signed off. This is *the* official record of the production process.
Heat Penetration Study	Testing the sterilisation process when loaded with typical items, to check whether tightly-packed or sealed objects are still sterilised correctly

HEPA Filter	'High efficiency particulate air' filter, a filter which removes 99.97% of all particles that are 0.3μm and larger.
Hold Time	A potential pause in the production process, it is not always required but provides time to fix any problems which may occur.
Intervention	The process of doing 'anything' which is not part of the normal production process within the aseptic zone.
Isolator	A large protective shell which protects the production line from the surrounding clean-room. It can be closed or open, depending on requirements, and has the same cleanliness as a critical zone.
Leak Testing (filters)	In-place testing of the filter and its housing to ensure that it is working correctly.
Mapping Study	A study to check if the sterilising equipment and process leads to equal temperature and pressure throughout the entire system.
Master Batch Record	The not-yet-filled-out record containing instructions for all steps in the production process.
Media Fill Study	A 'practice' run of your normal production/filling process using microbial growth media, to check whether everything comes out sterile.
Membrane Filter	A polymer membrane with tiny pores that block microbes/particles. Can be used for liquids or high-pressure gases.
Passive Air Monitoring	Checking for the presence of airborne microbes by leaving an open agar plate out for a few hours.
Process Characterisation	The act of performing numerous tests on your manufacturing process to see what variations lead to which changes in the final product or result.

A Glossary of Terms

Process Validation	Proving (and documenting) that your process is highly reproducible and leads to a high-quality final product.
Qualification	Testing and documenting that the equipment is capable of acting as it should.
Sterilisation	Killing everything! Everything microbial, at least.
Sterilisation Assurance Level	The probability that a sterilisation run will fail and leave living microbes behind.
Terminal Sterilisation	Producing the drug product in a clean but not aseptic fashion, then sterilising the final sealed product via heat or irradiation. Usually not appropriate for biological therapeutics.
Trending	Checking to see if testing results, even if still within specifications, are drifting towards being out-of-specification.
Validation	Checking your processes to see if they consistently work as they should.
Worst-Case Load	Used in autoclave validation, this is a full load of difficult-to-sterilise objects.

About the author

Originally from the sunny shores of Australia, CF Harrison currently works in the beer-filled heart of Bavaria. With a PhD in biochemistry, he has worked in drug discovery, as a scientific consultant, and as a regulatory affairs manager for a major international pharmaceutical company.

After being asked many, many times just what people meant with all this talk about media fill studies (and why anyone should care), he decided to answer these questions once and for all – and thus this introductory book was born.

Those interested in contacting him can drop a line to lifeafterlifescience@harrison-scientific.com.

Other books by the author include:

Pharmaceutical Regulatory Affairs: An Introduction for Life Scientists

Available on Amazon in eBook and Print formats

www.ingramcontent.com/pod-product-compliance
Lightning Source LLC
Chambersburg PA
CBHW061227180526
45170CB00003B/1195